Atomic LOVE

Other Books by Dani Zyp:

Blossoming Like Flowers 2011
    out of print
Sacred Touch 2013
    available on amazon.ca
The Book of Women's Mysteries and One Man's Confusion 2015
    available Audrey's Books
Nude Poetry 2017 (with Ronald Kurt)
    available Audrey's Books

ATOMIC LOVE

Copyright © Belly Button Books, 2023

All rights reserved. No part of this publication may be reproduced, stored in a retrieval system, or transmitted in any form or by any means, electronic, mechanical, photocopying, recording, or otherwise, without written permission of the author and publisher.

Author photo by Tammy Watson

Editor: G. Zenska

Published by Belly Button Books, Edmonton, Canada

ISBN:
- Paperback   978-0-9739781-8-6
- ebook   978-1-7388985-0-3

Publication assistance and digital printing in Canada by

PageMaster.ca

Dedicated to Moms and Dads
with everlasting love around the world

Chapters

Meditation I 1
War & Peace 11
Choose Peace 19
Family Love 27
Atomic Love 41
Romance 53
Meditation II 61

Index 66

Chapter One
Meditation I

IF IT CAN BE WELL

If it can be well
and I have felt the pain vacillate
into wellness
then it can be well all the time

Meditate on green
healing colour of the heart
sit back and imagine
a healthy green world

Growing and ever expanding
OOOOOOOOOOOOOOOMMMMMMMMMM.
    (PLAY TIBETAN SINGING BOWL)

EVERYONE COUNTS

Every stone

Every feather

Every day
In all kinds of weather

Every leaf
Every flower bud
Every moment
Now or never

We are all one
With joy!
Until you are happy
We aren't better

Every person
Every breath
Everything matters
And everyone counts.

LOVE IS ALL AROUND US AND WITHIN

The emptiness I feel when I'm alone
Is something I just can't condone
I need to feel spirit
Love I need to hear it
In the poems and the music I write

Stillness can really heal the heart
Being one is not really all alone
We are one with spirit
In my writing I hear it
Love is all around us and within

The stillness of the nothingness
Reaches in
Pulls out all the nasty toxins
Cleansing spirit
Eyes taste smell, I hear it
Love is all around us and within.

MY MEDITATION

My meditation starts with
Silence and passage of light
Grows into painting
Morphs into music
My meditation becomes this poem
Poetically divining spirit in motion

It is the start of a new year!
Time for new beginnings
Making new habits good habits
Like no cigarettes or at least less
And stretching and yoga every day
Eating healthy and sleeping well

CONTINUED...

Even more important is the decision
To actively encourage reciprocity in relationship
Avoid the abusers and users
The ones who ask for too much and give too little
Narcissistic sycophantic sadistic creeps

This year – I am free!
To wander and meander through my memories...
Find a true meaningful expression
Channel the creator
Become the maker.

TREES HAVE A SECRET LIFE

Trees have a secret life
You can hear them
Whispering in the wind
Rustle of leaves
Roots growing underground
The sound they say
"I am alive –
Breathing"
Even in the dead of winter
Springtime a dream

Trees provide oxygen
Life-giving love
Lines of the branches
Texture of the trunk
The sound they say
"I am warm –
I hear you
Tell me your heart's desire
Make your wishes come true"

CONTINUED...

Trees are inspiration
Artists' delight
Energy spirits
Even in the stark days of winter
Sunlight shining colour
A palette pink green yellow blue
The sound they say
"Open your heart –
Reach out
Let the snow outline
Our deep stained-glass beauty."

SHADOW OF LACE

Live in bliss and blossom
Like a hibiscus flower opening
To the sun
A philodendron growing immense
Leaves, light
Shadow of lace
On its skin.

Chapter Two
War & Peace

WILD FREEDOM

You are cold
And I have your sweater
You come running
Running running
Toward me with
Wild freedom
In your eyes
The desire for warmth
Me to comfort you
Wrap you in love
Cocoon you and
Fill you up – until
You are full with rapture

Rare bones casting
Shadows intricate

CONTINUED...

Angel of love
You are empty
I have your heart
You come running
Running running
Wild freedom
Streaming through your hair
Loose, long, curls astray
Fall into my arms
Soft and warm
Tears falling
As love wells up
In your heart
Beating to a rhythm
Of your own
Tum-tum, tum-tum, with mine.

I'M NOT AFRAID OF NUDITY

I'm not afraid of nudity
I walk naked within cloths of illusion
To warm my bones in winter's frozen effect
In summer only to protect
Oooozing orifices
What do we do with the issue of nude breasts?
Or portions of curvaceous loveliness displayed
Like the curve of her cheek
To be looked upon with burning love and cool respect

                                  CONTINUED...

Sizzling memories that give us utmost exquisite torture
We can only act upon it with a consensual acquiescing
      – Yes –
When there is no question of our mutual desire
To engage to mend to reflect
Together our mutual admiration
Our deep undying love
Our touch a melting of muscle and skin
Reaching a flame within – primal –
Starting at the beginning of time
And dwelling within us with a rrrrummmmbling
That emerges as a need for children
A love of babies a love of people – the planet –
Living environmentally friendly
A complete world love
That grows exponentially every time we make love
All of us together in a cosmic love celebration
Healing the planet with every thrust
Every nuzzle every kiss every squish every time we make love
We are nude in our souls.

CALM – STORM – CHAOS

As I look upon the dog
Lazily relaxed in my lap
My friend beside me groaning with delight
As I rub both his neck and the dog's
I realize we have made peace
A certain kind of peace

Like the triplet of paintings
I created called "Calm – Storm – Chaos"
Our relationship has stewed and brewed
Suffered calamity thru to ecstasy
Like sailing on a glass water lake
Storm cloud threatens
We create chaos
Stirring up water and sky
Churning – tumultuous

Moments later – serenity with deep-felt peace
A two-hour meditation on
Relaxation and breath
A walk through fallen leaves
Spicy scent
Kicking up excitement
Threatening skies
Lapis lazuli shining with bright sun
Making each leaf its own beacon
Yellow and orange light
Letting us know there are joyful
Reasons to live
Our world is worth saving
Create peace.

Chapter Three
Choose Peace

FOREVER HUG

Forever hug
You held for me
Is always on my mind

No one else was there for me
Not that they don't care for me
They just weren't anywhere near me

You were near me
Across the bridge, climbing up the stairs
You were near me
And were aware of my deep needs

Forever hug
You held for me
Is always on my mind

                                        CONTINUED...

You held your body close to me
A friend of warmth and love
On a cold night, alone and afraid
You took away the mocking
Believed in what is real

No one understood me
They beat me up
They called me crazy
Except you
You imprinted yourself on my soul

Forever hug
You held for me
Is always on my mind.

LET THEM SHINE

Let them shine
Stars in a night sky
On a clear time
And rain pearls of wisdom

When clouds of love get in the way
Let magic shine
Like diamonds
Shine like diamonds

Raindrops shaped like diamonds
Our tears fall – evaporate

As each soul is rise
As each soul is rise
As each soul is rise

Sweet children
Born perfect
And perfect will be perfect again
Surrounded in love.

WHITE FEATHER WALKS WITH THE WIND

Hush now
Gold is friendship
Always choose love

Aboriginal woman
Whispers magic
To my inner ear
And after all these years
I feel you
And hear you
And keep pressing you
To my bosom
My heart
My inside self communes
With your inside self

CONTINUED...

The Creatrix – she knows
We have walked
Sacred ground together and
We are blessed
And cleansed in sweet grass
Both wet and dry

And have no shame or blame
And share
A depth of love
Through our experiences
Surpassing limits unknown
As the wind brushes
The palettes of our lives
Souls touching souls together in truth.

I AM RELEASED

I am released
I release myself
Quiet by the creek
I go down to pray
To do the right thing
To set my soul free I fold my hands
And ask a question
Looking for an answer
To my call.

Chapter Four
Family Love

THE FLOW OF ONENESS

To be always in love's embrace
To live fully and in the moment
To catch sadness
Allow it to be
Embraced as in a massage
Rub the knot gone

The not-gone-ness of your impending death
As sweet memories of you
Inspired moment to moment
Images of Ganesh and incense
Warm oil and loving touch

CONTINUED...

I wonder if you took the world
On your shoulders
As we all do
From time to time
But with you it was a revolution –
Rebellion against current systems
Reaching for understanding of
New thought from the ancients

You are a mountain meadow
Full with wildflowers
A stream of clear water
Moving in the flow
Of oneness…

I LOVE YOU

Daddy, I'm crying out to you
How much I love you
I'm infusing you with my love with every hug

Crying today after
Seeing you with intense oxygen
Close to heart failure the doctor said

Shedding tears, like memories of us, streaming
Thoughts of you always being there
Such a strong man, vital with gusto for life

Celebrate whenever you can is your motto
And we celebrate every sip of water
You have taught us the value in every step

I remember when you had a mane of grey hair
In love with Mom and standing so tall and true
Pensively happy as well as a raucous lively humourist

CONTINUED...

Today you had that beautiful
Beautiful twinkle in your eye
"I love you" I squeezed your hand
So fragile now and bruised
From bloodwork and needles
I melted down when I got home
To see the change in you physically
But so very blessed to see
The look of life in your eye
Pulsing, twinkling beaming love
Humour and intelligence
What you are beyond the physical
To your essence
Which will forever live on.

MAGIC

Magic happens
And I miss you
Disappearing items
Of no consequence
Appearing items
Of importance
The red ink – suddenly
In one stroke turning blue
The leaves turning golden
Then brown
Eventually new sprouts of green

You had such a green thumb
I always thought you were magic
In your majestical kingdom
The purple shamrocks
Giant shining sun
I think of you

CONTINUED...

Your magic finger
Your magic thumb
Your magic twinkle in your eye
Gleam of love
A deep magic in your soul
You believed it was all a miracle
Painting and poetry channeled
Straight from God and Goddess
With your beautiful hand
For lettering and brush strokes
Your touch as tender
As a baby with a wisp of feather
Cherished lines of wisdom
And humour – as you would have
Trumped Donald Trump
And Jason Kenney with
Reasonable insanity from the
Libertine left
Your exaggerated cartoons and wit I miss you today
A deep hot magical rhythm of love.

WHITE TULIPS

We are bending in the arms of time
Cradled by our memories
Lilting in the windless rustle of leaves falling
The frozen snowflake memory of you forever

I am honoured to view this beauty
This cherished gleam of love in your eyes
Reflected in light surrounding me
With the warmth of the people in every "glimerous" sunset
Triangular
Shapes
Of memories shifting shapes
Shapes shifting shapes and colours
Images of you forever embedded
Impressed upon me
The look of you
The sound of you
The feel of you...

                              CONTINUED...

I remember you always happy
And ready for celebration
Even within your contemplation
Poetic words and tears of compassion
Always willing to help
And loving us all equally well
I keep you next to my heart
Always beating with love
In this tiny pocket of you
Sealed in sterling silver
Leaves and flowers being the
Embodiment of my memory of you
You said:
"Always remember me as a field of white tulips"
Shining through
Sunlight and shadow
With love
Enduring afterlife love
I love you.

A MOTHER'S LOVE

My Mother holds the memory
The all-important memories
To keep a child-like innocence
Sparks of joy on the human eye
A sense of wonder to keep me spry

Hungry to eat more love
Thinking with love and soul
A purity that keeps me whole
Enveloped and knowing true love
Makes everything grow

I search and continue to seek
To find the one cup
The two cups
The deep cups deeper deeper

                                                CONTINUED...

Reaching turgid waters where the treasures
Of the drownings created eternal life

When I awaken by the fire with my true loves'
Worship and waiting and worthy
To make holy the temple
To be released and able again together
Make love like saving souls
Saving souls
Created from earth and fire
Communion with stars
Holy molten lava transforming
Evil yearnings to essential ephemeral essence

Real goodness
Real pleasure
Knows no bounds
When lightening thoughts strike and abound
Eternal truth is making love into ecstasy
Ecstatic ecstasis.

THANK-YOU

You are a pillar of strength
In my life
Solid and weight-bearing
Floating and light

We laugh and cry together
Each from a different era
Communing when it is sad
Outrageous or funny

Coming together
From such opposite places
We share meals, stories
And living spaces

                                                        CONTINUED...

I learn from you every day
As you learn from me

I would have to plumb
To the bottom of the ocean
To fathom how deep
Is our love

As you are in the winter
Of your years
I remember you young and energetic
We share our memories
You are my friend, companion and Mother –
I'm so happy to call you Mom. Thank-you.

LOVE EMBERS

Oh blood moon divine
Glowing red with love embers
Ties that never die.

Chapter Five
Atomic Love

HEAD SPACE

Clear and lucid In the morning
Before the
Detritus of the day
Fills my spaces
Drink cool clean
Water, so easy to get
From the tap
Don't have to go
To no water well
I am lucky to have
This place to run
To when home is
Unfriendly. This place
Has always been a space

                                      CONTINUED...

For people running away
Today I will write,
Rehearse music
And visit my
Grand nephew who is 2
Many of my favourite
Things today so I
Am well enough to
Recognize my incredible luck
And just to stay safe
And create
Whatever you want
Each day a clean slate
To start again and make manifest your dreams
No rehearsal required!

SUN'S DEEP RAYS

Enjoying sun's deep rays
After days and days
Of quixotic scent of
Heavenly lilacs
Frothy Mayday blossoms
Priming myself for
Linden trees and honeysuckle
Delicate tulips stand at attention
Spring is in the air
Floating in elm seeds
Swirling on the ground
And nesting in nooks and crannies.

WRITING FOR MY LIFE

I'm just a drop in the ocean
Writing, writing, writing for my life
Wave upon wave of untold stories
Tumble from my mouth
My gut, my soul, my spleen,
In every drop of my saliva
My pen remembering so fast I can barely catch up
With the ink to the thoughts

I start to write in shorthand
And skip huge segments
Running, running, running for my life

CONTINUED...

I'm writing, writing, writing
Stories buried within my healthy marrow
Embedded upon my third eye
A jewel of brilliant flashes
Returning to love
Enveloping, rapturing, saturating
Every pore with honey nectar quixotic

Running, running, running
To a retreat of writing, musical, loving, nurturing women
To let the stories catch themselves and
Be allowed to unfold without
Repeating, repeating, repeating
Until you ask yourself: Are you done with that?
What are you doing here in this material world
When a spirit is waiting in a warm wrapped cocoon
Ready to encapsulate you into ecstasy.

SISTERS OF MERCY

Leonard Cohen is my man
An endless romance
Started with girls tearing their blouses off
At bars in Mexico, lo, so many years ago
morphed into going down
with Suzanne
where I found heroes amongst the garbage
and the flowers
I learned how to touch his body with my mind
I was in a distance relationship:
A mellifluous mind-fuck with Leonard Cohen
Hallelujah!
I began bathing in the moonlight on the roof
There were no diamonds in the mine
Because I finally went clear...
Hallelujah
Sisters of Mercy -save me
Leonard Cohen waltzed me
To the end of time.

UNDER A SNOW MOON

The moon is following us
Shapeshifting moonshine
Eternally there
Lit by the light of the sun

Oh, living in a swimsuit
Under a snow moon
Family in the freezer
Friends in flames

The sun is coming up
The moon is going down
Will they ever meet and marry?
Reaching across the sky

Oh, living in a swimsuit
Under a snow moon
Family in the freezer
Friends in flames

CONTINUED...

No, they will never be together
Each trapped in a revolution
Beautiful symmetry
Yet totally opposite

Oh, living in a swimsuit
Under a snow moon
Family in the freezer
Friends in flames

Happiness mixed with sorrow
Sunshine through the rain
Smiling at the moon
Sun crying in pain

Oh, living in a swimsuit
Under a snow moon
Family in the freezer
Friends in flames

Forever together
Forever apart
Forever together
Forever apart.

ATOMIC LOVE

Talking about the consciousness of disease
How much is in our heads
Our brains, our perception

There is a physical limit – boundary –
In this realm
We are all atomic energy
To the core

When we're in love
We merge at an atomic level

Imagine circular bubbles
Coalescing
Fingers of love
Feeling each other

Nodes of knowingness
Nuzzling each other

Little love licks
Tickling each other

CONTINUED...

Love is a perception

An inner pulsing
Fire of love
Pushing, pulling
Yearning, learning
Fire of love
In the brain
In the heart
The inside webbing between the fingers

Love burns eternally
Universally
We are bound
To merge and emerge
Meld and mingle
Positive compounding exponential love atoms

I was talking to him
About the consciousness of disease
How love is the answer.

Chapter Six
Romance

FLOATING

Missing summer
Floating falling leaves
Autumn
Glorious, exquisite little death
Every day golden orgasms
Falling floating whipping
Leaves crunching

May cold never chill the soul
May sun forever warm the bones
Smear salve on the wounds.

IN YOUR EYES

I floated in your eyes
Inside the heat of images
Wild horses stampeding
Wild rice growing
Wildness in your eyes

Together with you
I see intricate filigree
Resonant picture of you running
Action of young boy-girl innocence In your eyes.

WAVES OF THE SEA

Waves of the sea
Ebb and flow
I talk to you
In a dream
Ebb and flow into
The now

One forlorn flower
Pokes out of
The freshly fallen snow
Reminding us
Of sunshine and summer

The lonely
Wind-blown tree
Poetic
Like all of us
Ultimately alone

I feel your wild spirit
Take hold of me
With desire
Want to hold you

CONTINUED...

In my arms
By the fire –
Wrap myself in our magic
I hunger for your touch
As I touch myself
Reaching deep
For your stories and poetry

It's your liquid eyes
I could fall into and
Never leave

Wish they were magic and
It will be
You will go dancing
With faeries and me
Across the ocean
Across the sea
I feel your love
Beating to me.

TANGERINE NIPPLES

Luscious protrusion
Intrusion upon
My lusty senses

I peel you
With my tongue
Lips longing
To suckle

Your juices
Dribbling
Down my chin

Sweet intoxication.

SPRING STORM

(PERFORM WITH HARMONICA)

Letting the breeze blow
In the big city
Centre of the heart
Boys blowing their engines
Leaving for the weekend
Lakes and sunset sea-doo's

Fall is coming already
And I'm weeping tears
Like a tree weeps leaves
Kaleidoscope of colour
Reaches inside my mind
It is spring inside
Peonies and roses blooming
Scent of honeysuckle and new possibilities
Each petal opening a new thought

CONTINUED…

Leaves tremble
Oscillating shadow and light
My meditation melancholy music
Tickles my ears
Laughter through tears
Sends poetry to my fingertips
Writing from darkness to bright
Negativity feeding positive outcomes
A storm is brewing electricity
Pulsing
Our hands entwined
Lightning rips the sky
Flashing our eyes
Wind blowing
Rain wetting our faces
Counting 1 2 3 4
Crackle thunderous
Rumbles reverberating our hearts.

Chapter Seven
Meditation II

ON OUR WAY HOME I

Our spirits are cleansed,
Mended and repaired
Even though
Our bodies are breaking down
We think positive
Thankful for what we have found

A sunny day shining through the window
Enjoy rays of love bestowed upon us

As our bodies break down
The mind remains
Causing twinkles in our eyes
When family takes time with us
We like to see our children
Children of any family
The world family

CONTINUED...

We carry forth
Soldier forward
Enjoying the golden moments
Realizing a life lived
Lives on in the memories we make today
As yesterdays morph and mingle
Into todays and tomorrows
Lived on through youth and
The love imprint we impress upon each other's souls
We carry other souls with us
On our way home.

ON OUR WAY HOME II

On our way home
We fall into a contemplative silence
Both dreaming our journey
Toward health
The winding lanes with weathered gate
Huge archways to pleasure
As our golden years find ways
To encourage miracles of emotion
Memories where we lofted on God and Goddess breath

Scent of baking and soft cuddly blankets
Our minds making dreams
Of future love-making
Giving and receiving
An equitable oscillation
Tessellation, orientation, equation
Our common goals:
Outstanding human rights for women
Causes friction with men of any race
Women: shaping and shifting
Creating spaces for love
Shape shifting and creating
New personas

CONTINUED...

To be women who grow and develop
Loved and loving
North American poverty is such
A difficult state of being
Put yourself in Burundi
No more third world and first world
One world
In a spirit of unity
Cooperative
Working together
Taking spiritual action towards
An overwhelming volcano of spilling forth world love
One Love.

Contents

A MOTHER'S LOVE 36	MY MEDITATION 5
ATOMIC LOVE 50	ON OUR WAY HOME I 62
CALM – STORM – CHAOS 16	ON OUR WAY HOME II 64
EVERYONE COUNTS 3	SHADOW OF LACE 9
FLOATING 54	SISTERS OF MERCY 47
FOREVER HUG 20	SPRING STORM 59
HEAD SPACE 42	SUN'S DEEP RAYS 44
I AM RELEASED 25	TANGERINE NIPPLES 58
IF IT CAN BE WELL 2	THANK-YOU 38
I LOVE YOU 30	THE FLOW OF ONENESS 28
I'M NOT AFRAID OF NUDITY 14	TREES HAVE A SECRET LIFE 7
IN YOUR EYES 55	UNDER A SNOW MOON 48
LET THEM SHINE 22	WAVES OF THE SEA 56
LOVE EMBERS 40	WHITE FEATHER WALKS WITH THE WIND 23
LOVE IS ALL AROUND US AND WITHIN 4	WHITE TULIPS 34
MAGIC 32	WILD FREEDOM 12
	WRITING FOR MY LIFE 45

To order more copies of this book, find books by other
Canadian authors, or make inquiries about publishing your
own book, contact PageMaster at:

PageMaster Publication Services Inc.
11340-120 Street, Edmonton, AB T5G 0W5
books@pagemaster.ca
780-425-9303

catalogue and e-commerce store
PageMasterPublishing.ca/Shop

Dani Zyp

Dani started to write stories at the tender age of five illustrated by her own artwork. Supported by family and friends she continues to publish, participate in readings at various venues and write new words; always with art in process. She worked for many years as a professional writer in tv/film/radio and journalism. As well she has invested significant time, energy and money into a professional art practice and currently facilitates an art class with the Wellness Network.

Under the pen-name Dani Zyp, this is Dani's fifth book of published poetry with covers of her own painting on four of them. She has contributed to several anthologies one of which became an Edmonton number one best seller, which is for sale at Audrey's Books - and other works from volunteer newsletters to employment for prime time television in major centres like Melbourne, Australia to Vancouver, B.C. Young at heart Dani recently further developed her call to art with soul-work writing and performing original music and playing harmonica.